This Book Belongs To:

BY
Home Planners And Journals

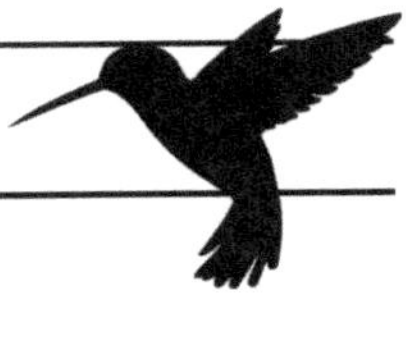

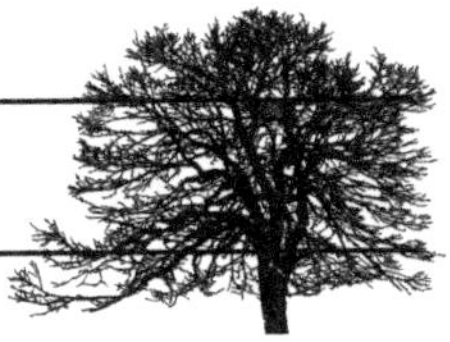

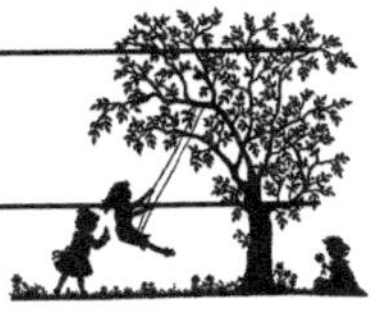

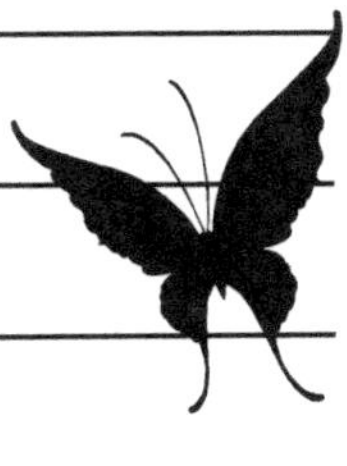

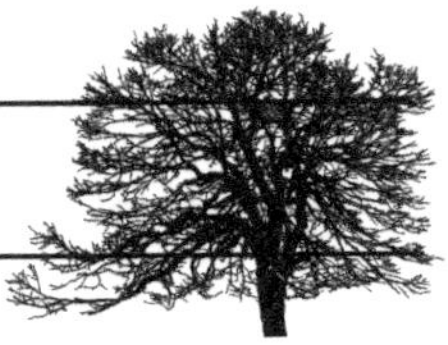

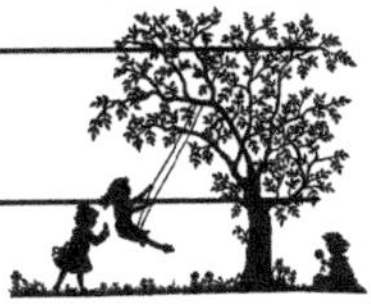

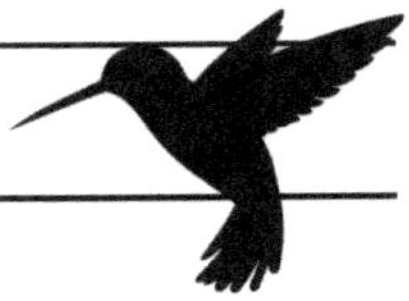

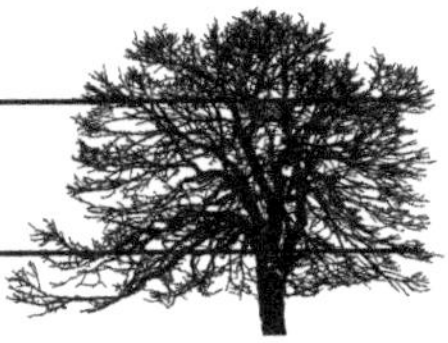

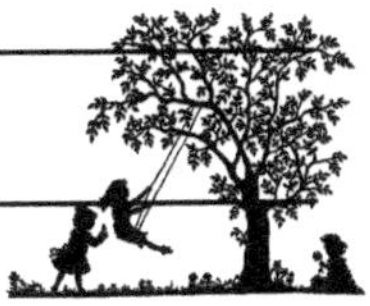

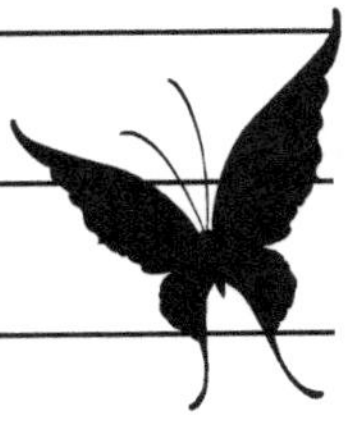

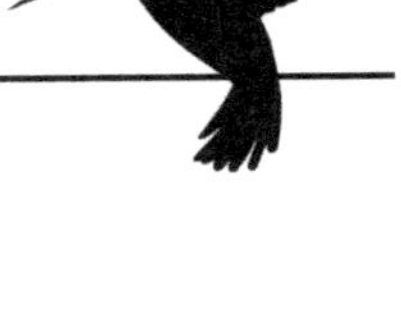

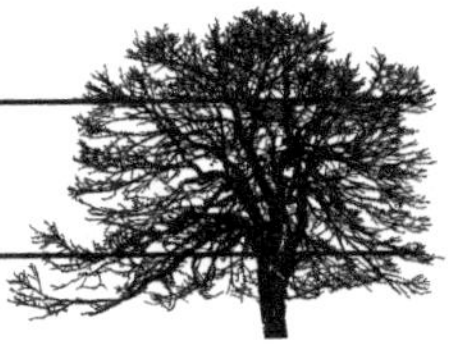

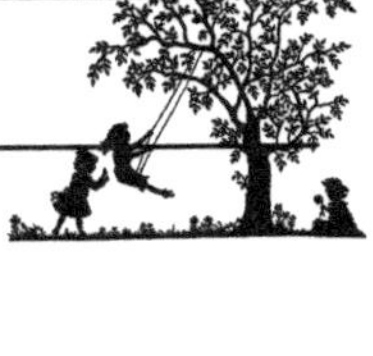

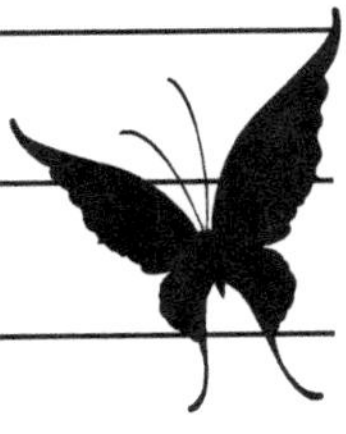

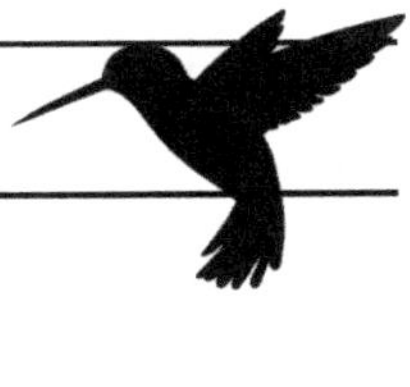

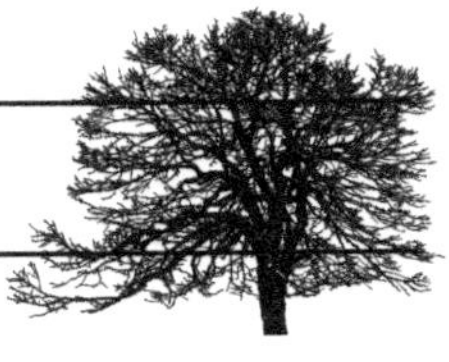

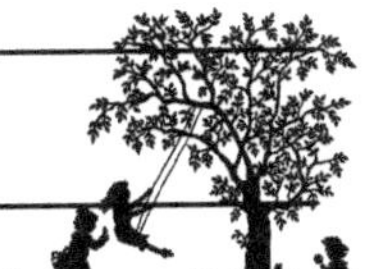

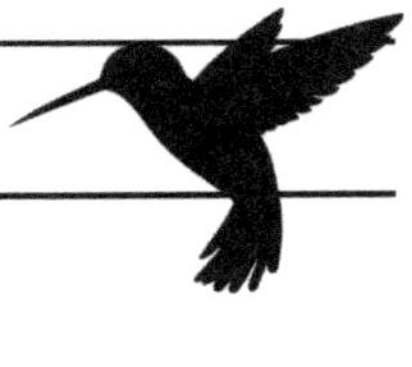

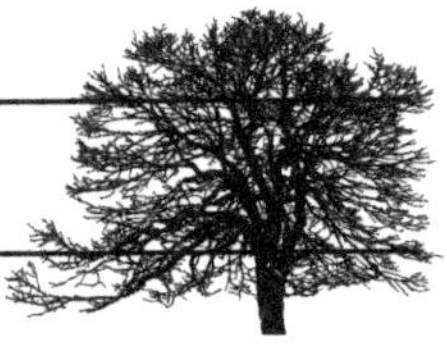

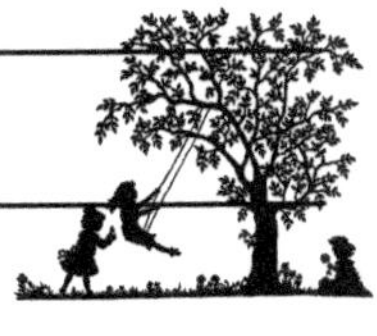

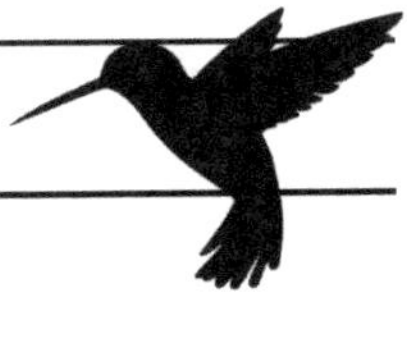

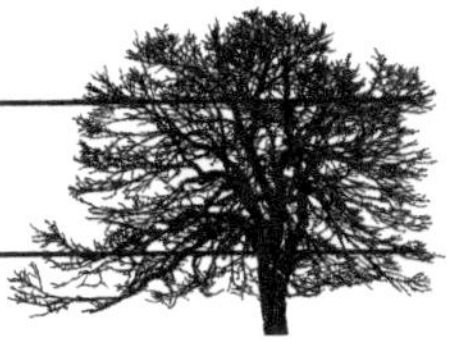

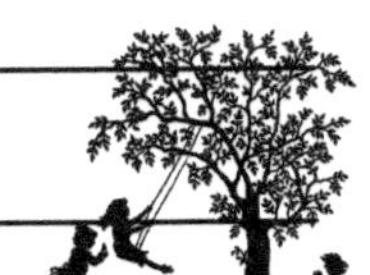

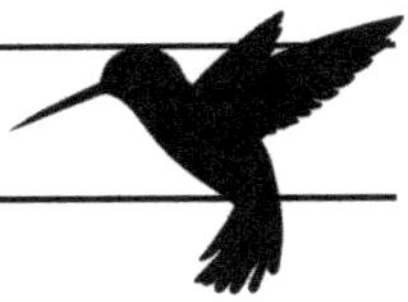

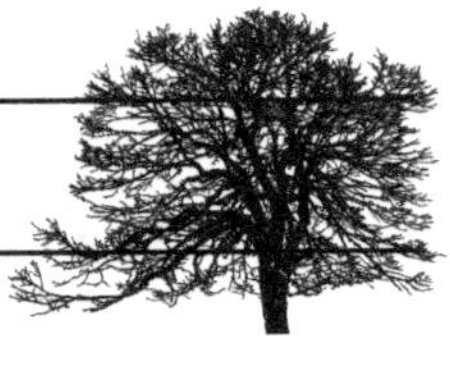

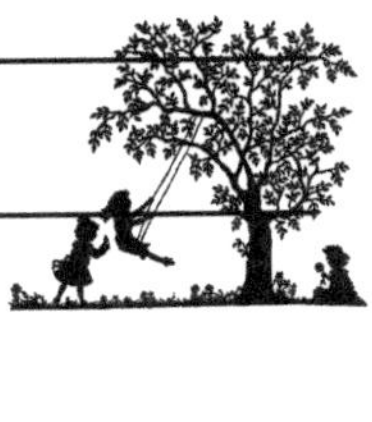

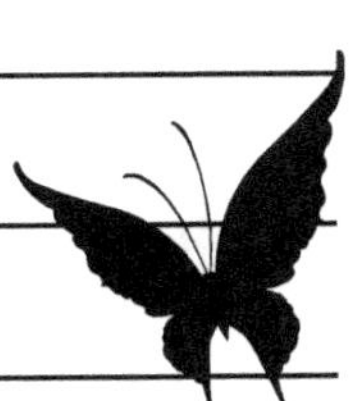

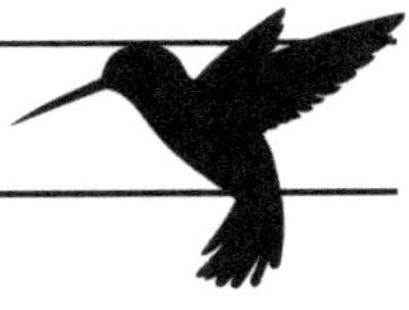

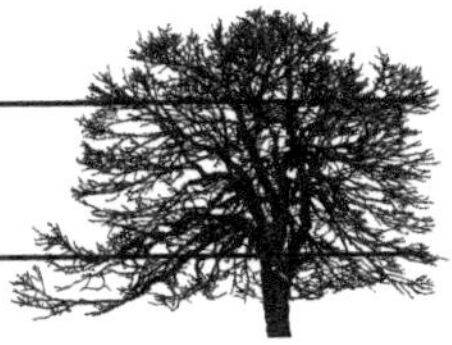

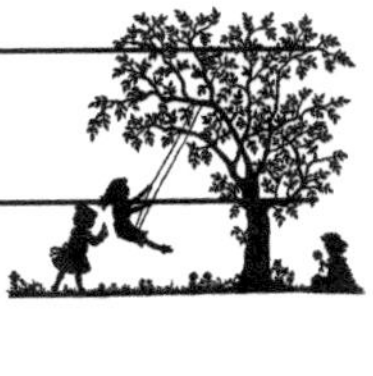

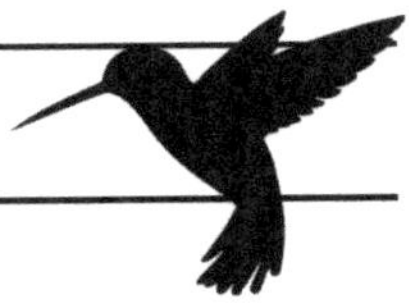

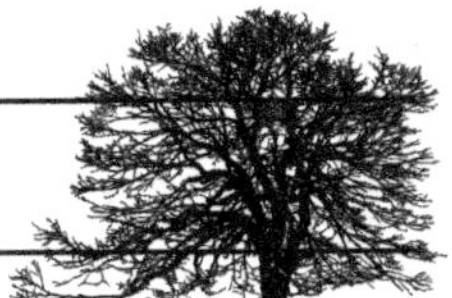

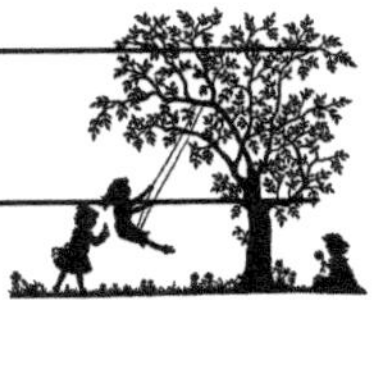

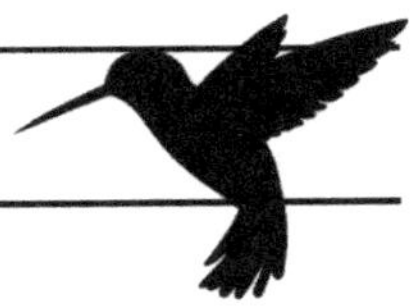

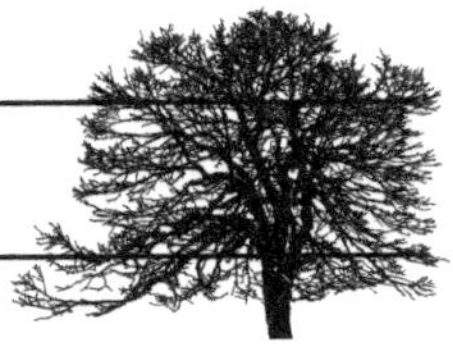

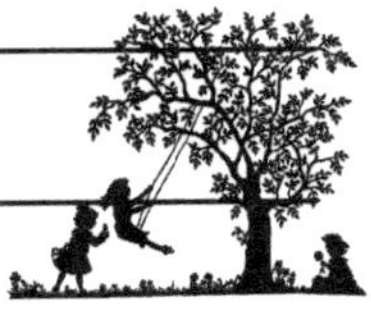

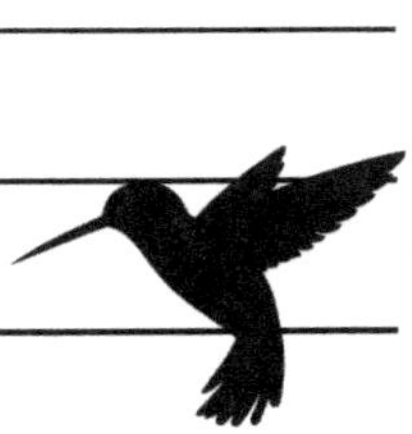

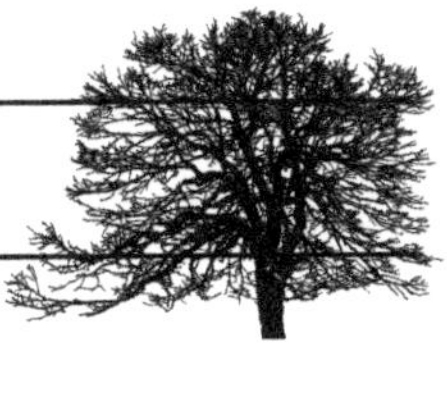

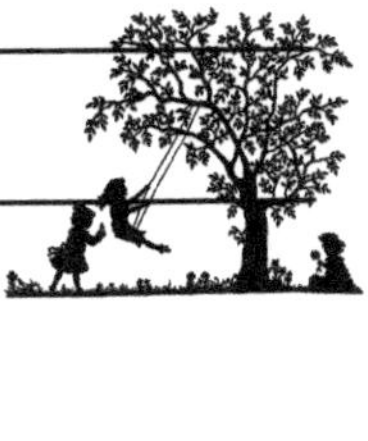

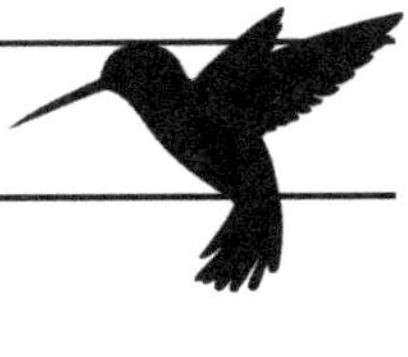

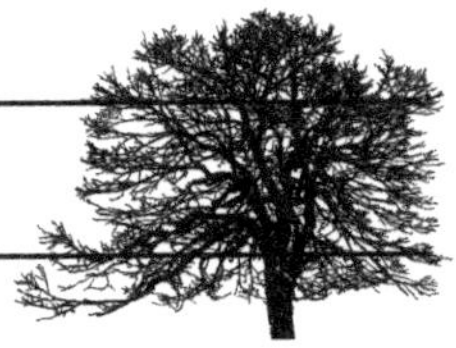

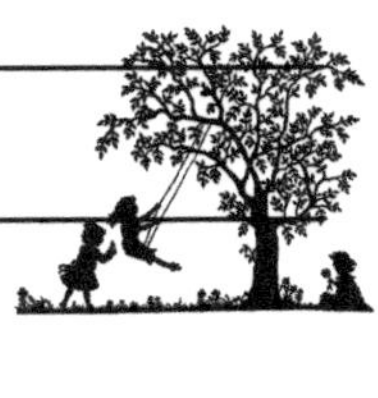

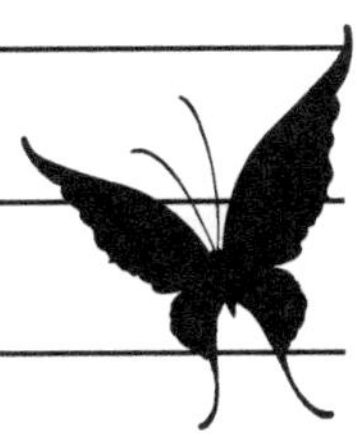

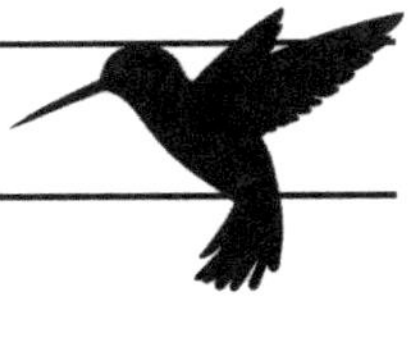

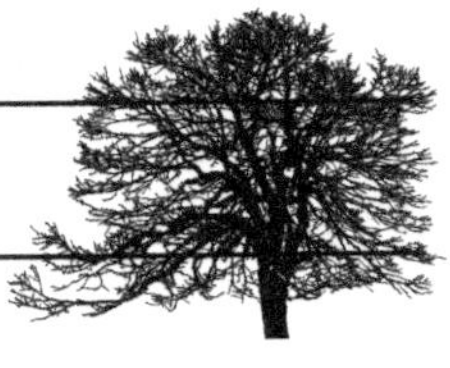

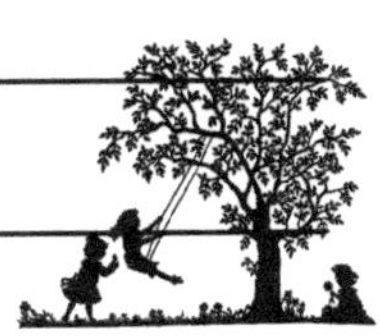

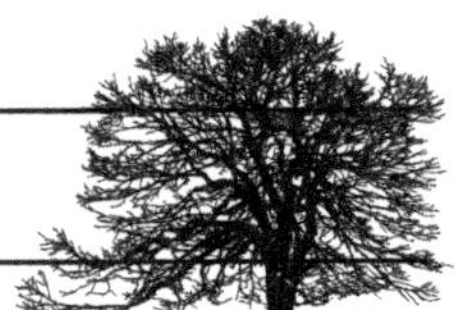

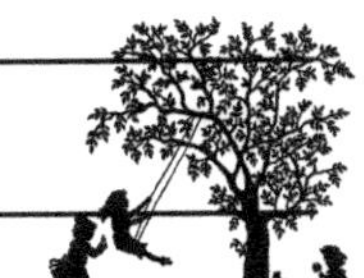

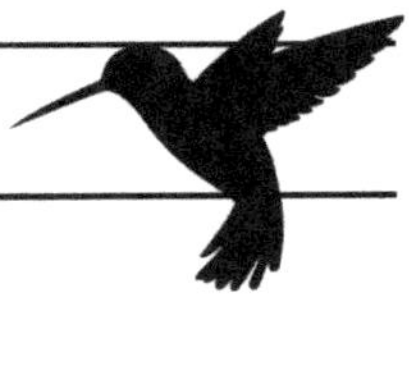

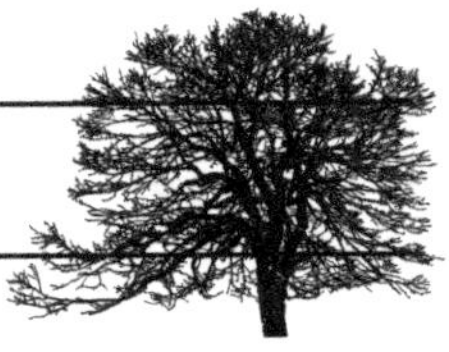

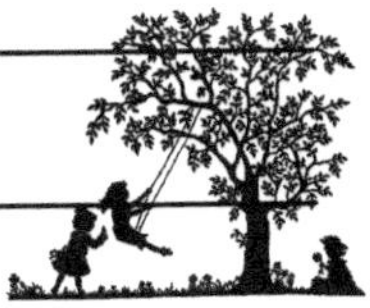

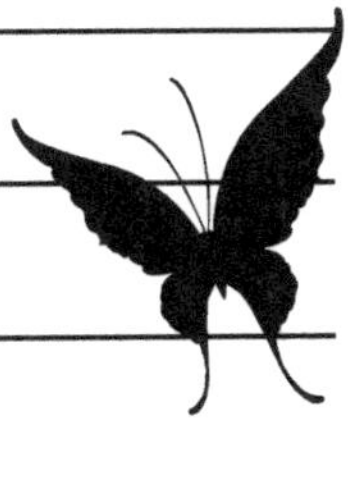

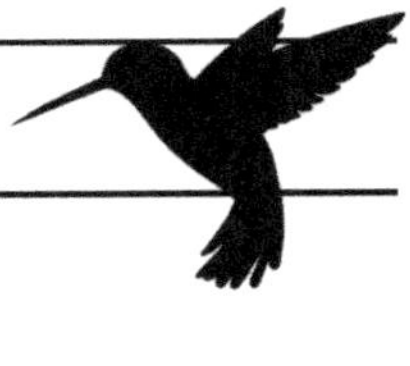

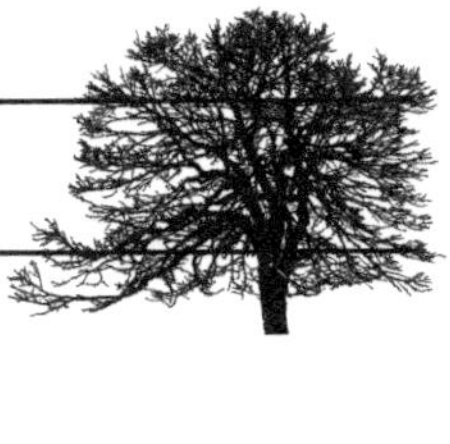

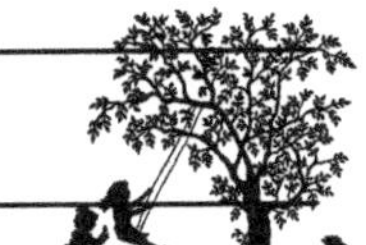

www.ingramcontent.com/pod-product-compliance
Lightning Source LLC
Chambersburg PA
CBHW072052280526
45788CB00006B/2262
* 9 7 8 1 0 9 0 2 3 5 9 7 8 *